FORENSIC FILES

INVESTIGATING FAKES & HOAXES

. . . . . ALEX WOOLF . . . . .

www.heinemann.co.uk/library
Visit our website to find out more information about Heinemann Library books.

To order:
 Phone 44 (0) 1865 888066
Send a fax to 44 (0) 1865 314091
 Visit the Heinemann Bookshop at www.heinemann.co.uk/library to browse our catalogue and order online.

First published in Great Britain by Heinemann Library, Halley Court, Jordan Hill, Oxford OX2 8EJ, part of Harcourt Education. Heinemann is a registered trademark of Harcourt Education Ltd.

Editorial: Sarah Eason, Georga Godwin and Kate Bellamy
Design: Jo Hinton-Malivoire and AMR
Picture Research: Rosie Garai and Andrea Sadler
Production: Edward Moore

Originated by Ambassador Litho Ltd
Printed and bound in China by South China Printing Company
The paper used to print this book comes from sustainable resources

ISBN 0 431 16025 2
08 07 06 05 04
10 9 8 7 6 5 4 3 2 1

British Library Cataloguing in Publication Data
Woolf, Alex
Investigating Fakes and Hoaxes
001.9′5
A full catalogue record for this book is available from the British Library.

Acknowledgements
The Publishers would like to thank the following for permission to reproduce photographs:

ACO Electronics Ltd p. **7**; Boijmans Museum p. **18**; British Library p. **10**; Corbis p. **23** (Pablo Corral); Corbis/Bettmann p. **31**; Corbis/Hulton-Deutsch Collection p. **26**; Foster Freeman p. **35**; Harcourt Education Ltd. p. **6**; Hulton Archive p. **12**; Gareth Boden pp. **11, 25**; Getty p. **8** (Mansell); Indigoimage.com p. **24** (Zoe Feast); John Frost Newspapers p. **28**; National Gallery of Canada p. **20**; PA Photos p. **34**; Peter Kurth pp. **13,14**; Rex Features p. **16**; Science and Society p. **9**; Science Photo Library pp. **5, 22** (Michel Viard/Peter Arnold Inc), **17** (Mehau Kulyk), **21** (Matt Meadows/Peter Arnold Inc), **27** (Robert Holngreen/Peter Arnold Inc), **32** (Geoff Tompkinson), **33** (Klaus Guldbrandsen), **39** Volker Steger/Peter Arnold Inc), **41** (Dr P Marazzi), **42** (Blair Seitz); Stern Magazine p. **30**; SWNS p. **38**; Topham/PA p. **37**; Topham Picturepoint p. **40**; Wellcome Photo Library p. **29** (Sophie Scott).

Cover photograph of a painting by Lucas Cranach the Elder (1472–1553) seen under ultraviolet light reproduced with permission of Science Photo Library/Volker Steger.

The Publishers would like to thank Peter Bull and Nicola Greene for their assistance in the preparation of this book.

Every effort has been made to contact copyright holders of any material reproduced in this book. Any omissions will be rectified in subsequent printings if notice is given to the Publishers.

Disclaimer

Contents

Any words appearing in the text in bold, **like this**, are explained in the Glossary.

What is forensic science?

Forensic science is any science used in a criminal **investigation**. Its purpose is to provide scientific evidence for use in a court of law. Forensic science draws from a number of different subject areas: mostly chemistry and biology, but also physics, geology, psychology (study of the human mind) and social science (study of people in society).

What do forensic scientists do?

In a typical criminal investigation, scene-of-crime officers will gather material evidence from the crime scene. Forensic scientists then examine this material for evidence to be used in the investigation and the trial. This can be anything from the body of a murder victim to the tyre tracks of a getaway car. Forensic scientists do not spend all their time in laboratories and offices. They are often called to attend crime scenes, or to appear in court as expert witnesses.

Investigating fakes and hoaxes

Investigating crimes involving fakes and **hoaxes** can involve a number of different forensic skills. The services of a forensic document examiner will usually be called upon. But fakes and hoaxes do not always involve paper and ink. In one case study in this book, a recorded voice is analysed to check if it is that of the person it is supposed to be. In another case, involving a fake painting, **X-rays** are made of the canvas to find out what lies under the painting. When a hoax involves a murder, forensic scientists may be asked to examine the body of the victim.

Investigator's toolbox

Forensic document examiners have a number of scientific techniques at their disposal when analysing a **questioned document**:

1 Paper analysis: paper has a number of physical and chemical properties that can be investigated. For example, the fibres making up paper can be identified by examining it under a microscope. The most powerful microscopes, such as electron microscopes, can tell an examiner what kind of wood was used to make the paper, and even what species of tree it came from!

There are also very sensitive measuring devices for testing the differing densities (concentration of matter) of paper. This can help, for example, in determining whether a watermark is genuine or not.

2 Ink analysis: sometimes forensic document examiners run tests on ink, to discover for example what it is made of and how old it is, or to reveal writing that has been erased or scribbled out. A technique called **thin-layer chromatography** enables scientists to separate out the different ingredients of ink to help identify it. The age of ink can be discovered by measuring how far certain ingredients, known as **solvents**, have evaporated. Erased or written-over ink can often be seen by looking at the document in **infrared** light. Viewed in this way, certain inks appear luminescent (very shiny), while others appear dark. This process is known as **infrared luminescence**. It can also be used to distinguish between different inks that appear the same in normal light.

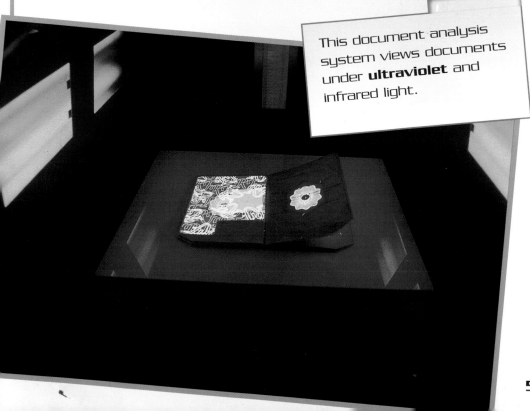

This document analysis system views documents under **ultraviolet** and infrared light.

Forensic science – in action today

The bank manager studies the cheque, but he can find nothing wrong with it, except for the odd amount. The signature on the cheque looks like the signature held in the bank's records. Yet, according to the person on duty, the man who paid the cheque in to the bank seemed nervous. The bank manager decides to hand the cheque over to the local police. The police, in turn, pass the cheque to a **forensic** document examiner.

Looking for clues

The document examiner's office is full of microscopes and **X-ray** machines. Yet when she is handed the cheque, she first uses her own eyesight. The human eye is better than any technical device at picking out things that seem odd or out of place. The examiner has the cheque photographed alongside an accurate measure. This is to keep a record of the cheque's appearance, in case any of her later tests alter or damage it. Then she asks the bank to provide her with a handwriting sample from the person who holds that bank account.

A different hand

An examination of the size and quality of the paper confirms that the cheque itself is genuine, and her tests on the ink show that the same pen was used for all the writing on the cheque. However, under the microscope she can see something odd about some of the words and numbers. Certain parts have clearly been written more slowly with a different

Each person's handwriting has its own individual characteristics.

pen pressure, and with different starting and connecting strokes. She soon realizes that the cheque was originally made out for nine pounds, and that the extra words and numbers have been carefully added in. The police are told, and later that day, the man who presented the cheque is called in for questioning. A **fraud** has been uncovered, thanks to the work of a forensic document examiner.

Questioned documents

The work of a document examiner may not seem as exciting as that of a detective on the trail of a murderer, yet documents can be dangerous. They can be used to mislead people, to take money from them, even to steal their identity.

Most cases of fakes and **hoaxes** involve **questioned documents**. A questioned document is any written, typed or printed item that a forensic document examiner studies to decide whether it is genuine. It can be anything from a **counterfeit** banknote to a set of falsified (deliberately altered incorrectly) business accounts, or a faked diary claimed to be that of a famous historical figure.

Forensic analysis can be carried out on paper, ink and handwriting, to establish such facts as the age of the document, who produced it and whether it has been altered. This has often provided the police with crucial evidence in cases involving fakes and hoaxes.

A questioned document is placed on a shelf beneath this video microscope, and the image is then displayed on the monitor for analysis.

Forensic science – the early days

The history of **forensic** science goes back to ancient times. Handwriting, for example, was studied by the ancient Greek philosopher Aristotle. There is also evidence that the ancient Chinese carried out autopsies (examinations of dead bodies to find out the cause of death). A Chinese book, *Hsi Duan Yu* ('The Washing Away of Wrongs'), written in 1248 tells how to distinguish drowning from strangulation. However, it is only in the last 200 years that science has played a major role in the fight against crime.

One of the first people to apply scientific techniques to the exposure of fakes and **hoaxes** was a Frenchman, François Demelle, who in 1609 published the first essay on **questioned document** examination. Around two hundred years later, in Germany, the first recorded chemical test for a particular ink dye was carried out. In 1910, Albert S. Osborne, who was perhaps the most respected forensic document examiner in history, published his landmark work, *Questioned Documents*.

Seeing more clearly

In 1622 Camillo Baldi of Italy wrote the first scientific book about the study of handwriting. The in-depth scientific study of documents, including their paper, ink and handwriting, could not have happened without the development of equipment to assist vision. The first-known microscope was built in the 1590s by Zacharias and Hans Janssen in Holland. Over the next centuries the power and focusing capabilities of microscopes were improved dramatically.

In 1828, William Nichol invented the polarized light microscope, which allowed scientists to analyse transparent materials in far greater detail than was possible before by measuring changes in the quality of

In 1894 Alfred Dreyfus was trapped into writing an incriminating letter. This was used to prove him guilty of handing military secrets to the Germans. He was pardoned in 1906.

light passing through them. In the 1850s came photomicrography, enabling scientists to take photographs of what they saw under their microscopes. The 20th century saw the arrival of **digital imaging technology**, allowing greater magnification of microscopic images.

X-rays and beta rays

Microscopes could magnify things, but could not show scientists what lay under the surface. For that they had to wait until 1896 and Professor Röntgen's discovery of X-rays. X-rays operate at a different **wavelength** to normal light waves, and are able to penetrate solid objects. For the first time it was possible to look at the structures within materials such as paper and paint.

Beta radiography was first developed in the 1950s. This method uses streams of electrons, known as beta rays. Beta rays can penetrate solid objects, but they do not penetrate powerfully, and are easily turned aside by things like the fibres within paper. This is why beta radiography is often used to examine **watermarks** in paper. The beta rays are passed through the paper on to a sheet of special film that is sensitive to these rays. More rays pass through the watermark because the paper is thinner there, and so the shape of the mark is imprinted on the film.

A 19th-century microsope.

The English author and engraver Samuel Ireland was an expert in the works of William Shakespeare. On Christmas Eve, 1795, he revealed something quite astonishing to the world: a collection of manuscripts (handwritten work) had come into his possession that, he claimed, were actually written by Shakespeare himself. They included a fragment of 'Hamblette' (*Hamlet*), and a complete manuscript of 'The Tragedye of Kynge Leare' (*King Lear*), handwritten by Shakespeare. There was also a copy of a previously unknown play called *Vortigern*.

Suspicion

The public were eager to believe that Samuel Ireland's discovery was genuine. However, a Shakespearean scholar named Edmond Malone was suspicious. He asked if he could examine the collection. On 1 April 1796, Malone published a 424-page book aimed at fellow scholars and Shakespeare enthusiasts on the work, declaring it a fake. He pointed out the spellings of certain words did not match the way such words were written in the 16th century.

Paper chase

Malone also made a **forensic** investigation into the paper on which 'Kynge Leare' had been written. He discovered that the manuscript contained pages with 20 different **watermarks**. He reasoned that Shakespeare, who was already rich and famous by the time *King Lear* was written, would have purchased as much paper of one type as was needed for the entire work. On the other hand, a person wishing to forge an Elizabethan play 200 years later would need to obtain scraps of old paper from wherever he could get them – for instance, from the flyleaves (blank pages) of old books.

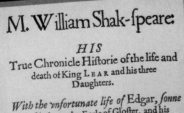

The frontispiece of a 1608 edition of Shakespeare's *King Lear*. Ireland claimed to have found the original manuscript written by Shakespeare himself.

In May 1796, Ireland's son, William Henry Ireland, published a book owning up to the deception. And in 1805, in another book of confessions, Samuel Ireland admitted that he had indeed paid a bookseller to let him cut out blank pages from the older volumes in his shop. The manuscripts had all been written by William Henry, who was only 21 at the time.

Watermarks

A watermark is an image set in a sheet of paper. These can be used to identify the papermaker, as each paper manufacturer creates its own unique watermark.

Watermarks are part of the structure of paper, embedded within its fibres during manufacture, and so it is virtually impossible to remove them or produce a convincing fake. This makes them very useful to forensic scientists in dating and identifying paper. Forgers have attempted to create fake watermarks by scratching the surface of the paper through a stencil with a hard eraser, but the disturbance of the fibres on the surface is easily detectable.

Another method involves printing the mark in olive oil, making the paper look translucent (allowing light to flow through) like a real watermark. However, the edges of marks made in this way are much sharper than genuine watermarks.

The **authenticity** of a watermark can be tested by **beta radiography**, which measures small variations in density in a sheet of paper.

Euro banknotes contain a watermark to make them harder to forge. The watermarks show a picture and display the value of the banknote.

20 EURO

Anna or Anastasia?

On 17 July 1918, the Russian Revolution claimed its most famous victims when Tsar Nicholas II of Russia, his wife Alexandra and their five children were murdered on the orders of Russia's new leader, Vladimir Lenin, at a house in Ekaterinburg, Siberia. As the hereditary ruler of Russia, the Tsar and his family could have provided the necessary leadership or figurehead for a movement to oust the Bolsheviks and restore the monarchy.

The woman in the canal

In February 1920, a woman, who had attempted to commit suicide, was fished from a canal in Berlin, Germany after jumping into the water. The woman could not identify herself, and she was taken to a mental home, where she remained for two years. In 1922, she claimed to recall who she was. She announced, to general astonishment, that she was in fact the Grand Duchess Anastasia Nicolaievna, the youngest daughter of the murdered Tsar Nicholas. The woman claimed that she had escaped the massacre with the help of a Russian soldier in the firing squad, named Tchaikovsky, whom she had then married. He was later killed, and she had suffered a mental breakdown, before making her way to Berlin, where she had tried to kill herself.

Anna Tchaikovsky. For two years after her rescue she was known as *Fraulein Unbekannt* [Miss Unknown].

These claims could easily have been dismissed as the ravings of a mad woman. There were several reasons why they were taken seriously. Firstly, the woman, who now called herself Anna Tchaikovsky, bore a remarkable resemblance to Anastasia. She also appeared to have an intimate knowledge of palace life and etiquette (rules governing polite behaviour). Furthermore, a number of witnesses who knew the late Tsar's family, including the family nurse, identified her as Anastasia.

Comparing photographs

In 1927, Professor Mark Bischoff of the Institute of Police Science in Lausanne, Switzerland, decided to carry out some tests to see if he could prove her identity. He compared photos of Anna Tchaikovsky with those of the duchess. These were adjusted in size and one was placed over the other for ease of comparison. Bischoff paid particular attention to the right ear, for ears have unique characteristics that can help with identification. There were some differences between the two. This suggested to Bischoff that they were not the same woman.

Ear identification

The examination of ears in identifying individuals was first proposed by a Czech doctor, R. Imhofer, in 1906. In 1964, an American deputy sheriff, Alfred Iannarelli, published a book called *Ear Identification* in which he created a classification system (a method of putting things into groups or classes) for the characteristics of the ear.

Iannarelli suggested that an individual's ear does not change throughout life, and, that everyone's ears are different. Iannarelli's theory remains controversial; not all experts accept that it has a scientific basis.

The National Training Centre for Scientific Support for Crime Investigation in the UK is now compiling a database of several thousand 'earprints' for use in identifying criminals. They claim that the **cartilage** (tough, elastic tissue) gives each ear its distinctive shape.

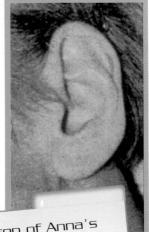

A comparison of Anna's (bottom) and Anastasia's (top) ears. Bischoff found differences between them.

Faked Pictures

In 1928 several American newspapers published photos of the young Anna Tchaikovsky taken in 1916, when she was 15 – so they claimed – looking remarkably like Anastasia. Bischoff studied these photos and proved them to be retouched copies of a genuine photo of Anastasia.

Supporters and sceptics

These retouched photographs of Anastasia appeared in American newspapers in 1928.

Several Russian aristocrats (members of the highest social class), who were forced to move and live away from Russia at the time of the revolution, supported Anna's claim. They hoped that she might encourage others to aim for a new Tsarist government, to replace the regime (governing body) at that time. However, there were many others who remained doubtful, including surviving relatives of the royal family such as Tsar Nicholas's mother and his sister, who may have feared that Anna might claim a share of the family fortune.

The doubters pointed to certain weaknesses in Anna's case, such as the fact that, although fluent in German, she only knew a few words of Russian – supporters argued that she had forgotten most of her Russian because of the trauma of her ordeal. Supporters pointed to the many physical similarities between the two women. For example, a finger on Anna's left hand bore a scar in the place where a carriage door had been closed on Anastasia's; there was also a scar on Anna's right shoulder where Anastasia had had a mole removed. Like Anastasia, Anna suffered from bone tuberculosis. She also recalled that her aunt, the Grand Duchess Olga, used to call Anastasia 'Shvipsik', a nickname only a small number of family members and staff would have known about.

A new name

By 1928, Anna Tchaikovsky had changed her name to Anna Anderson in an effort to avoid press attention, but the controversy (arguments) raged on. Over the following decades, she spent time in two mental hospitals, and went to court three times in attempts to prove that she was, in fact, Anastasia. In 1968 she married one of her supporters, John Manahan, and moved to Charlottesville, Virginia, USA, where she died in 1984. During her lifetime she convinced many who met her of her story, but was never officially accepted as Anastasia.

So who was she?

If Anna was not Anastasia, then who was she? As early as 1927 a theory began to circulate that Anna Anderson was in fact a Polish-born housewife named Franzisca Schanzkowska, who had been reported missing in Berlin on the same day that Anna was fished out of the canal.

This theory was first proposed by a private detective, Martin Knopf, who pointed out several similarities between Schanzkowska and Anderson. According to the medical records, in addition to the similarities mentioned above, both women had a history of foot disorders. Knopf also located a witness — Doris Wingender, daughter of Schanzkowska's landlady in Berlin — who was willing to identify Anderson as Schanzkowska.

However, Schanzkowska's brother Felix refused to accept that Anderson was his missing sister.

The evidence of DNA

Arguments about the true identity of Anna Anderson continued after her death. In 1985, a new identification technique was developed that promised to solve the mystery once and for all: **DNA typing**. Just before she died in 1984, Anna Anderson had undergone an operation, and the hospital had retained a sample of her tissue. The **DNA** in this tissue could be compared to the DNA of the Romanovs (the Tsar's family) to see if there was a family connection. But what was needed was DNA belonging to the family.

Finding the Romanovs

This became a possibility in 1991, when some bodies were unearthed from a shallow grave possibly where the Tsar and his family were believed to be buried. The first task was to prove that these were in fact the remains of the Romanovs.

Pavel Ivanov, a Russian DNA expert, took the bones to Britain to be examined by the Home Office **Forensic** Science Service, headed by Peter Gill. DNA analysis confirmed that five of the nine skeletons recovered were members of one family. To make a more specific match, the researchers turned to a different test, called **mitochondrial DNA** typing. By these means it was proved beyond doubt that these were the bones of the murdered Romanov family.

Missing bodies

Only nine bodies were recovered, however, although eleven were known to have been shot. The DNA typing showed that the two missing bodies belonged to Crown Prince Alexei and his sister Anastasia. Perhaps they had escaped. This news raised the

Peter Gill, whose team carried out the DNA tests on the Romanovs, is holding a photograph of Anastasia.

hopes of Anna Anderson's many supporters. They approached Peter Gill and asked him to test the sample of Anderson's tissue to see if it matched the Romanovs' DNA.

Mystery solved

In June 1994, Gill flew to the USA in secret to collect the sample. He also obtained DNA samples from members of the Schanzkowska family to see if there was any truth behind the theory that Anderson was actually their missing relative. The following October, he announced his verdict. Anna Anderson was not Anastasia. He could confirm that she was without doubt the Polish peasant woman, Franzisca Schanzkowska.

Not everyone has accepted this verdict. Many of Anna Anderson's supporters have rejected the scientific evidence, and continue to insist that she was the missing Anastasia.

DNA typing

DNA is a kind of molecule found in every **cell** of every living thing. Our DNA carries information about ourselves. It's what determines our physical characteristics, and it's what makes us exactly what we are — which is why it is useful for establishing identity. Scientists can examine chunks of DNA, lifted from blood, hair, skin or tissue, to find out who someone is, or whether they are related to someone else. This is called DNA typing.

On this photograph, the pieces of DNA are shown as dark bands, like a supermarket barcode. Different prints can be compared to find a match.

DNA from the **nucleus** of a cell is fragile, and is often hard to read when it comes from old bodies. A more stable source of DNA is found in the mitochondria — the part of a cell that produces its energy. However, mitochondrial DNA can only indicate maternal (mother's-side) relationships.

Possibly the greatest art forger of all time was Hans van Meegeren (1889–1947). Not content with copying a great painting and trying to pass it off as the original, van Meegeren actually created original works of his own, and sold them as new discoveries of old masters. As well as his own work, van Meegeren specialized in forging the work of fellow Dutchman and celebrated artist, Johannes Vermeer (1632–75).

Fooling the experts

During the 1930s van Meegeren faked six Vermeer paintings in all, giving them titles such as *The Washing of Christ's Feet*, *Christ and the Adulteress* and *Lady and Gentleman at a Spinet*. Most famous of all, and generally considered to be van Meegeren's masterpiece, was *Christ at Emmaus*. This painting was bought for a considerable sum by Boymans Museum in Rotterdam in 1937.

Christ at Emmaus. This is the faked painting that van Meegeren showed to Abraham Bredius.

The art historian Abraham Bredius wrote about *Christ at Emmaus* in the *Burlington Magazine* in 1937: 'It is a wonderful moment in the life of a lover of art when he finds himself suddenly confronted with a hitherto unknown painting by a great master, untouched, on the original canvas, and without any restoration, just as it left the painter's studio! And what a picture! ... [W]hat we have here is a – I am inclined to say – *the* masterpiece of Johannes Vermeer of Delft.'

A victim of his own success

During World War II, van Meegeren sold another 'Vermeer', *Christ and the Adulteress*, to **Nazi Reich Marshal**, and art collector Hermann Göring. In May 1945, he was arrested and charged with treason for having sold a Dutch national treasure – a Vermeer painting, no less – to the enemy. After six weeks in jail, van Meegeren announced that he himself had painted the 'Vermeer', and had in fact conned Göring with a fake. Not only that, but he had painted five other so-called 'Vermeers'.

How he did it

Van Meegeren went to great lengths to make his paintings as authentic-looking as possible. For *Christ at Emmaus* he followed this procedure:

1 He obtained a genuine 17th-century painting with its original stretcher (the wooden frame over which a canvas is stretched).

2 He painted over the original artwork, preparing a fresh surface, which he used for his own painting.

3 Once the painting was complete, he used an ageing process he had invented, which fooled all the experts. He ground his **pigments** in oil of lilacs and then mixed them in a particular kind of resin dissolved in a colourless oil called turpentine.

4 He then baked the painting for several hours at a temperature of over 100°C.

The effect of this procedure was to give the work the appearance of a genuine 17th-century painting.

Prove it!

Van Meegeren's announcement was greeted with amazement and disbelief. To prove his claim to the court, in autumn 1945 van Meegeren was locked in a room, with a police guard and six witnesses, to paint another 'Vermeer'. After two months in the room he produced another excellent Vermeer forgery, *Young Christ*.

Forensic tests

This was still not enough to convince many experts, and the court called for a **forensic analysis** to decide for certain whether van Meegeren was telling the truth. In June 1946, Dr P. B. Coremans, director of the Central Laboratory of Belgian Museums, was called in. He carried out extensive physical and chemical tests on a number of paintings and materials found in van Meegeren's studio. Coremans found that van Meegeren had used paints containing traces of cobalt blue, an artificial pigment not available until the 19th century. **X-rays** also showed original 17th-century pieces under the paintings.

X-ray analysis

X-rays are rays made of the same **electromagnetic** particles as light, but with a much shorter **wavelength**. These shorter wavelengths allow

An X-ray photograph of a painting.

X-rays to pass through solid objects, such as the surface of a painting, to show what lies beneath. Radiographers (X-ray specialists) are often called upon to authenticate works of art. To investigate the van Meegeren forgeries, Coremans used a kind of X-ray process called **stereoradiography**, which operates at the same wavelength as doctors use to see inside the human body.

Imprisonment

In September 1947, Coremans reported that the paintings were indeed forgeries. The treason charge was dropped. However, the revelation produced anger and dismay in the art world, as Göring had not been the only customer to be taken in by the faked Vermeers, and van Meegeren had made a great deal of money out of his deception.

What was more, he had made fools of several well-known art experts. In October 1947 van Meegeren was tried and convicted of forgery, and sentenced to a year's imprisonment. He died of a heart attack two months later.

Analysing the paint

Paint is made up of various parts, such as pigments, extenders (substances that dilute or add body to a product) and binding media (materials that make pigments stick to a painted surface). A forensic scientist can study these components (parts) in order to reach conclusions about the date or origin of a painting because some components would not have been available before a particular time in history, and their presence or absence therefore helps to date a painting.

Today, forensic scientists can use techniques such as **gas chromatography**, a process that separates a substance into the parts that go to make it up.

Coremans used the tools available to him, such as a polarized light microscope (PLM). A PLM analyses changes in the quality of light passing through a sample of paint, and by doing so can give clues to identity.

This forensic chemist is looking at the results of gas chromatography carried out on a paint sample in a 3-D graph.

Counterfeit currency

Fabio Mendes began his **counterfeiting** career in 1970, working out of a friend's house in Bogotá, Colombia. His friend operated a small printing press, which he used to run a legitimate (legal and honest) printing business during the day, producing leaflets, posters and stickers. At night it produced US hundred dollar bills, which Fabio then sold on the streets of Bogotá.

Making money

During the late 1970s and early 1980s, Fabio's counterfeiting business took off, and over the years he sold fake hundred-dollar bills worth several million dollars. He was part of a large industry: between 1985 and 2000, over a hundred million dollars of Colombian counterfeit dollars passed into circulation.

Paper and ink

For counterfeiting, the materials and equipment are very important. For paper, Fabio used dollar bills, because they had the right weight and texture. Using bleach, he washed them clean of ink. Some counterfeiters saved money by using Venezuelan bolivar notes. Yet Fabio took pride in his workmanship, preferring to pay more for paper of the right quality.

This **forensic** scientist is checking the **authenticity** of paper currency.

Inks also varied in quality and price. Many counterfeiters were content with the cheapest inks. But these could smear easily. Fabio preferred to spend more on special magnetic and security inks, similar to the ones used to print real dollar bills. These inks could cost over 750 dollars per kilo.

The security strip

The security strip that ran through hundred-dollar bills also presented a challenge to Fabio. But he painstakingly threaded a metallic material between the two thin sheets that were used to make up the bill. 'The guy who doesn't include that security strip won't get anywhere,' said Fabio to a journalist from *The New York Times*.

The printing process

Fabio used a traditional method of printing, known as **offset printing**:

1 He created actual-size photographic negatives of the front and back of a hundred-dollar bill.

2 With great care, he cleaned up each negative.

3 When they were ready, the images on the negatives were burned on to a series of light-sensitive aluminium plates. A light is shone through the non-image areas of the negative that burns itself onto the light-sensitive solution that covers the aluminium plate.

4 The plates were attached to the printing press, and the bleached one-dollar bills were run through the press.

Fabio was prepared to waste a lot of paper at the start of a run, working to get the ink levels right. 'After that,' he said, 'it's like making bread rolls.'

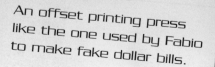

An offset printing press like the one used by Fabio to make fake dollar bills.

Traditional values

During the 1990s, many commercial printers began to swap their traditional methods for **digital scanners** and computers. But Fabio continued to use mechanical printing methods. This was partly because of the high cost of computer equipment, but also because the outstanding craftsmanship of his work would be difficult to match using computers.

Beating the counterfeiters

In 1996, the United States Treasury attempted to strike back at the counterfeiters by introducing a new range of high-tech elements to their bills, making them harder to copy. They used an '**optically variable ink**', for example, that appeared either black or green depending on which direction you viewed it from. The new bills also included a larger portrait (incorporating more detail), a **watermark** and **microprinting**. There are several methods of microprinting. In one, a **laser** beam is focused on paper covered with a thin metal film. The laser beam burns the metal causing it to bond with the paper and a printed pattern forms.

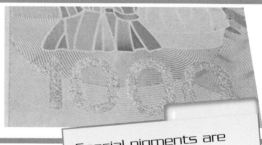

All these changes made Fabio's job much more difficult. Watermarks, for example, were impossible to copy exactly and microprinting details were very difficult to achieve.

Special pigments are used in optically variable ink, so that the colour changes if you observe it at an angle of 30 to 40 degrees.

Public trust

By 2000, Fabio was no longer producing fake bills, but worked in the multi-million-dollar distribution industry that moved the counterfeit money from the producers in Colombia, to New York, Miami, Buenos Aires, Tokyo, London and Madrid. He admitted to *The New York Times'* reporter that life was harder these days for counterfeiters. Still, the one factor counterfeiters always had on their side was the public's trust in the notes they carried in their wallets. Very few inspect their money closely enough to observe whether it was real or fake. Fabio had not been caught at the time of the interview in 2000.

New technology

Science and technology have been used in various ways to make currency harder to counterfeit:

1 Optically variable ink: it looks green when viewed straight on, but black at an angle — colour-shifting ink was used in the numeral in the bottom-right corner of some notes in the US 1996 redesign.

2 Microprinting: to the naked eye it appears as a thin line on many of the 1996 bills, but under a magnifying glass the lettering can easily be seen. Yet most offset printers or copying machines are unable to copy the detail of such fine print.

3 **Holograms**: a new anti-counterfeiting idea that is being introduced around the world is the addition of a 3-D hologram using advanced reflective foils.

Holograms are an expensive, but highly effective security feature. The image changes according to the angle of viewing, and multiple colours are often used.

One day in 1971, a writer named Clifford Irving approached the McGraw-Hill Book Company with a literary sensation. He announced that he had been granted permission to write the biography (life story) of Howard Hughes, the world-famous multimillionaire, movie-maker and eccentric. The publishers were amazed. Hughes had not been seen in public for years, and there had been several rumours of his death. Irving showed them a letter that he said was written by Hughes, giving him access to talk to the great man. The editors at McGraw-Hill were convinced by Irving's story, and the letter, and paid him a massive sum of $765,000 (£475,000) for the right to publish the book.

The perfect subject

In fact, Irving had never met Hughes. He had dreamt up the whole story, and forged the letter himself. Irving had calculated that Hughes, being both famous and invisible, was the perfect subject for this scheme. On the one hand, the public was hungry for information about him, and on the other hand, no one could deny the biography was genuine.

During his research for the book, Irving came across a copy of Hughes' handwriting, and used that as a basis for his forged letter. On two separate occasions, McGraw-Hill hired graphologists (handwriting experts) to check the **authenticity** of the handwriting (this was after they had already agreed to publish the book), and both experts concluded that the letter was indeed written by Hughes.

Irving told McGraw-Hill that Hughes also required payment for the book, and the publishers sent regular cheques to Irving

Clifford Irving claimed that he had met Howard Hughes more than a hundred times to tape-record his life story.

payable to H. R. Hughes. Irving's wife opened a Swiss bank account under that name and deposited the cheques.

Pure fiction

Irving delivered the 900-page manuscript, based – he claimed – on written records of lengthy telephone conversations between himself and Hughes. In fact he had drawn on magazine articles, and interviews Hughes had given during his more public years, mixed in with completely fictitious details. *LIFE* magazine believed it to be authentic and bought the rights to serialize passages from the book before it was published.

Handwriting analysis

Experienced handwriting analysts can spot differences between handwriting samples that look to most of us as if they are written by the same person. A person's handwriting has certain characteristics, which remain present throughout adult life. Someone attempting to copy that style may manage a superficial likeness, but on closer inspection differences will show up. Indications of disguised writing include:

- shaky formation of letters
- awkward pen movements
- stops and starts in odd places
- careful repair of wrongly formed letters.

It is easier to copy the overall shape of someone's handwriting than the details like pen pressure and connecting strokes which depend on the structure of the actual hand.

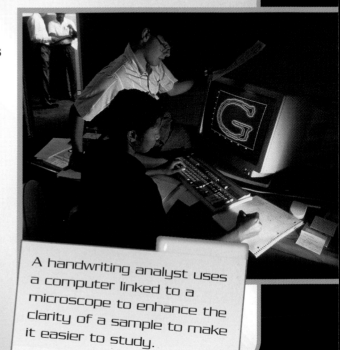

A handwriting analyst uses a computer linked to a microscope to enhance the clarity of a sample to make it easier to study.

Telephone conference

When McGraw-Hill and *LIFE* announced their '**scoop**', the real Howard Hughes was enraged. He was even prepared to break his fifteen-year silence so that he could personally deny any connection with the book. A telephone press conference was arranged through the broadcasting organization NBC (National Broadcasting Company). Hughes gave the conference from his luxury hideaway on Paradise Island in the Bahamas, to a group of reporters in a Los Angeles hotel.

The reporters' first task was to establish the authenticity of the voice on the other end of the telephone. The first questions were answered easily enough. Then one reporter reminded him of his round-the-world trip in 1938 when a woman placed a good-luck charm on his aeroplane. 'What was it,' the reporter asked, 'and where was it placed?'

There was a long silence at the other end of the phone. 'I have to be completely honest with you,' came the voice eventually. 'I don't remember that one.' But before the reporter could finish his next question, the voice interrupted: he recalled it now – the woman had stuck a wad of chewing gum to the tail of his plane. All the other reporters' questions were answered to their satisfaction, convincing them that they were talking to the real Howard Hughes.

Hughes then launched into a sustained attack on Irving's book. '... I don't know [Irving]. I never saw him,' he said. 'I have never even heard of him until a matter of days ago when this thing first came to my attention.'

A perfect match

When the telephone conference was made public, Irving immediately declared the caller an impostor, describing the voice

Newspaper headlines when Irving confessed. In June 1972, he was found guilty of forgery and was sentenced to 30 months in jail.

as 'much too vigorous and deep ...' However, NBC had expected this, and had hired **voiceprint** expert Lawrence Kersta to analyse the tape. Kersta found that it perfectly matched a recording of Hughes' voice in a speech he had made 30 years earlier to a Senate subcommittee. A second expert agreed.

Game over

From this point on, Irving's **hoax** began to fall apart very quickly. The Swiss banking authorities, suspicious of the woman in dark glasses who had opened the H. R. Hughes account, launched their own **investigation**. They handed documents containing handwriting, supposedly by Hughes, to the Crime Laboratory of the Postal Inspection Service in New York. After close examination differences were found between Hughes' handwriting and Irving's imitation of it.

Voiceprint analysis

The match that Kersta had found between the voice on the tape and Hughes' speech 30 years earlier proved his theory that although voices change over time, their special quality remains constant. His first task, when comparing the voices, was to convert the tapes into **spectrograms**, or voice pictures, measuring such aspects as pitch, tone and volume. He then compared the voice pictures from each tape line by line.

Voiceprint spectrograms can be viewed on computer screen, or as printouts. They show horizontal lines of constantly varying width that measure a voice's pitch, tone and volume.

A printout of a spectrogram, showing the basic patterns of pitch, tone and intensity that make each voice unique.

In February 1981, Gerd Heidemann, a journalist at the German magazine, *Stern*, handed the directors of the magazine's parent company, Gruner and Jahr, the publishing **scoop** of the century: the diaries of Adolf Hitler. Heidemann showed them three volumes, in black binding, filled with an almost unreadable German handwriting. He told them there were 27 volumes in all, covering the years 1932 to 1945.

The source

Heidemann did not reveal his source, except to say that the diaries came from a wealthy collector of Nazi memorabilia (memorable souvenirs) and brother of an East German general. Heidemann knew this man only as Dr Fischer, but his real name was Konrad Kujau, born in Saxony in 1938. A petty criminal and talented forger, Kujau had in fact written the diaries himself.

Consulting the experts

Despite the vagueness of Heidemann's story, Gruner and Jahr were prepared to trust him. They agreed to buy the diaries for around £1.25 million. Only then did Gruner and Jahr submit the diaries for **authentication**. The two handwriting experts they consulted both agreed that the diaries were genuine. This was not surprising as the 'genuine' samples of Hitler's handwriting the experts were given to compare the diaries against, came from the same source as the diaries: Konrad Kujau!

The first pages of the diary were published in *Stern* on 25 April 1983, the day Gruner and Jahr announced their scoop.

Gruner and Jahr began paying Heidemann huge sums of cash, for him to pass on to his source. Heidemann kept a lot of this money for himself, and began buying expensive cars and houses. However, none of his fellow journalists appeared to notice the rapid rise in his standard of living.

Media frenzy

Gruner and Jahr announced their scoop in April 1983, and the diaries instantly captured the world's attention. Historians considered how this might change completely our understanding of the Nazi leader. The magazine *Newsweek* competed with Rupert Murdoch's media empire for the right to publish the diaries internationally.

Murdoch asked the respected British historian and world-renowned authority on Hitler, Hugh Trevor-Roper (later Lord Dacre), to examine the diaries. Under pressure from the German publishers, he announced that, in his view, the diaries were genuine. Trevor-Roper later admitted he had been overwhelmed by the huge quantity of material placed before him. He had also been influenced by the fact that the handwriting had already been authenticated. Trevor-Roper thought the diaries were real, but he had been swayed towards that conclusion.

Gerd Heidemann (on the right) with Wolf Hess, son of Nazi leader Rudolf Hess, holding one of the notebooks of the Hitler diaries.

The forger

Konrad Kujau embarked on his criminal career in the 1960s, forging luncheon vouchers (vouchers given by employers to staff to exchange for lunch).

From there he went on to forging paintings and Nazi memorabilia, and ultimately the Hitler diaries. Kujau had convinced Heidemann that the diaries had been rescued from the wreckage of a plane carrying Hitler's personal property, which had crashed in Dresden in 1945. He told him the diaries had been secretly stored for over three decades by his brother, an East German general, before being smuggled into West Germany in the late 1970s.

Forensic enquiry

By the time Trevor-Roper reached his verdict, the West German authorities knew the diaries were fakes. Government **forensic** scientists had conducted their own enquiry into the diaries, concentrating this time on the paper and ink. Under **ultraviolet** light, the paper in six of the diaries was shown to contain a whitening agent called blankophor, which had not come into use until after 1954. The book bindings also contained whitener, and threads attached to the seals were made from viscose and polyester, both post-war materials. But the biggest giveaway was the ink. By measuring the evaporation of chloride **solvent** from the ink, the document examiners could establish that the 1943 diary had been written less than twelve months ago!

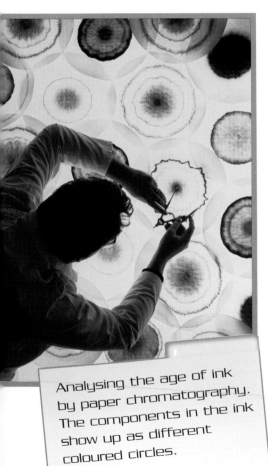

Analysing the age of ink by paper chromatography. The components in the ink show up as different coloured circles.

Trevor-Roper wrote an article for Murdoch's *Sunday Times* declaring his belief in the diaries. At the last moment, however, the historian began to have doubts. He called the paper, requesting the removal of his article, but he was too late – it was already being printed.

Exposure

On 6 May 1983, German government scientists announced that the diaries were in fact crude forgeries. For Gruner and Jahr this news was a financial disaster, costing them somewhere in the region of 20 million marks (10 million pounds). For Gerd Heidemann, who had been convinced all along that the diaries were genuine, it was a personal humiliation. It also meant his exposure as a criminal, as about 1.7 million marks of the fee for the diaries had found its way into his account. In 1985, he was convicted of misappropriating (using incorrectly) his employer's money, and received a prison sentence of four years and eight months. Konrad Kujau was sentenced to four years and six months.

Gathering forensic evidence

Forensic document examiners are often asked to identify and date the paper and ink on a document.

Analysing paper: a sheet of paper has many physical and chemical properties that can help to identify and date it. Most of the world's paper comes from **wood pulp** obtained by using chemicals to break wood down into its individual fibres. The fibrous (consisting of fibres) makeup of paper can be revealed by partially dissolving it in dilute acid and then examining the fibres under a microscope. The fibres have individual characteristics that can often tell you which wood they came from.

Ink dating: as ink ages on paper, a certain ingredient of the ink known as the solvent gradually evaporates. The rate of this evaporation can be expressed as a curve if drawn on a graph: it is most rapid when the ink is fresh, then it slows down and finally it levels off. Different ink types have different evaporation rate curves. One way of dating ink is to use **gas chromatography** to measure the quantity of the solvent, and then check this against the evaporation curve of that particular ink.

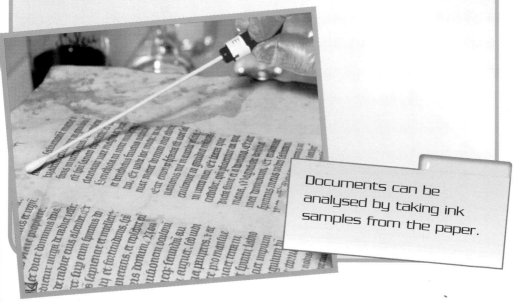

Documents can be analysed by taking ink samples from the paper.

Graham Backhouse was a failure as a farmer. Within a few years of taking over at Widden Hall Farm in Somerset, England, he had built up massive debts thanks to successive crop failures and his spendthrift ways. Not only that, but Backhouse – a married man – had angered his neighbours in the village of Horton, by openly flirting with several local women.

In March 1984, a sheep's head was found fixed on Backhouse's fence with a note attached: 'You next'. Backhouse went to the local police station, claiming this was merely the latest incident in a long hate campaign against him, including abusive letters and threatening phone calls.

The car bomb

On 9 April, Backhouse asked his wife Margaret to drive into town to pick up some medicine for his livestock. Her own car would not start, so she took her husband's car instead. When she started the car, a bomb, hidden beneath the driver's seat, exploded, causing terrible injuries to her thigh and thousands of deep, jagged cuts all over her body. Screaming with pain, she managed to crawl from the wrecked car. Backhouse failed to respond to her cries. He was some way off in the cowshed with the radio at full volume. Luckily she was spotted by some passengers on a passing bus, and was rushed to hospital.

Graham Backhouse, a 44-year-old former hairdresser, was an unpopular figure in Horton.

Explosives experts examined the wreckage and found evidence of a simple but deadly device. The bomb had been made from a length of steel pipe packed with nitroglycerine (explosive liquid) and shotgun pellets, and was wired to go off when the engine was switched on.

Threatening letter

Soon afterwards, Backhouse reported receiving another threatening letter. This note, along with the previous one, was sent to Mike Hall, a

Hall observed that each letter in the second note had been gone over backwards and forwards several times, making it impossible to identify the handwriting. When he turned his attention to the 'You next' note, Hall noticed the faint impression of a doodle on the back, probably made on the next sheet up in the notepad. He filed it away for future reference.

Analysing impressions

The impressions made by a pen pressing on paper can go through several sheets. To see these impressions more clearly:

1 cover the paper with a thin sheet of plastic, similar to clingfilm

2 give this sheet an **electrostatic** (stationary electric) charge. This creates an invisible electrostatic image on the sheet

3 pour black powder (toner from a photocopying machine) over the sheet, the static charge makes it stick to the image area

4 discard the excess powder, leaving a clear image of the marks made by the pen.

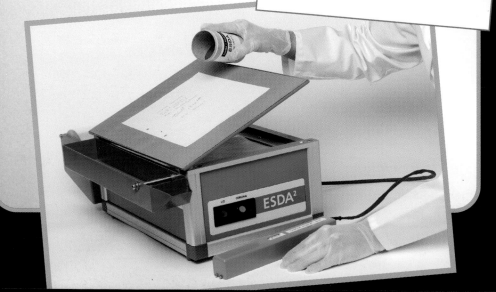

Black powder is about to be poured over this plastic-covered sheet of paper in order to reveal any impressions on the paper.

Trouble with the neighbour

Backhouse told the police that he suspected his neighbour, Colin Bedale-Taylor, of planting the bomb. The two men had been engaged in a lengthy dispute over a right of way, and 63-year-old Bedale-Taylor had been depressed since the death of his son in a car accident two years before.

Backhouse was given round-the-clock police protection at his farm. Nine days later, Backhouse ordered their removal, claiming he was quite able to defend himself. He had a shotgun after all. The police withdrew, warning him not to take the law into his own hands. An alarm button was installed at Widden Hall Farm, with a direct connection to the local police station. On the evening of 30 April, the alarm was sounded.

Knife attack

The police raced over, and found Backhouse just inside his front doorway, covered in blood. His face had been slashed several times down one side, and a deep gash ran from his left shoulder diagonally across his body. At his feet lay the dead body of Colin Bedale-Taylor, felled by two shotgun blasts. A bloodstained Stanley knife lay in the dead man's hand.

Backhouse described what had happened. Bedale-Taylor had come round on a neighbourly visit to enquire about Margaret's health. They were in the kitchen when Bedale-Taylor had suddenly gone mad, crying out that God had sent him. He admitted planting the bomb, but said it was in revenge for his son's death, which he blamed on Backhouse. He had then attacked Backhouse with the Stanley knife, and Backhouse had fought him off, before running to the hall to fetch his shotgun. Bedale-Taylor ran towards him, and Backhouse shot him, then shot him again.

The police were initially inclined to believe Backhouse's story. Further evidence was found to support Backhouse's description of events: the Stanley knife was engraved with the initials 'BT', and during a police search of Bedale-Taylor's house the steel pipe was found from which the car bomb had been made.

Crime scene analysis

However, certain odd features at the crime scene puzzled forensic scientists. For example, there was no blood trail between the kitchen and the hall, where Backhouse said he ran to fetch his gun. Also, Backhouse had no wounds on his hands. Such wounds are normally found on someone defending themselves from a knife attack.

Blood drops

The patterns made by drops and splashes of blood on walls, floors and clothing, can help forensic scientists build up a picture of events at a crime scene.

In the case of Graham Backhouse, it was noticed that the shape of the blood drops on the kitchen floor did not match with Backhouse's story.

During a fight or struggle, blood drops land with characteristic tails, yet these blood drops were simple round circles, as if they had dripped from someone standing still.

A Scene of Crime Officer investigates the pattern of blood stains found at a murder scene.

Stanley knife mystery

There was another mysterious difference: Bedale-Taylor, a carpenter, had engraved his initials with great care on all his tools, but the initials on the Stanley knife had been crudely and hurriedly carved.

Dr William Kennard was the pathologist (scientist who determines the cause of death) on the case. He was perplexed by the fact that the Stanley knife was found clasped in the fingers of the corpse, rather than lying on the floor. This could only have happened, he said, if rigor mortis (the stiffening of the body that occurs several hours after death) had taken place immediately – a physical impossibility. It was beginning to look as if Backhouse had killed Bedale-Taylor, and then placed the knife in his hand.

The wool fibre

Gradually, evidence built up to show that Backhouse had also faked the hate campaign against himself. An examination of the envelope containing the first threatening letter revealed a tiny wool fibre stuck to the gummed flap. This was carefully analysed, and was found to have come from Backhouse's own woollen sweater, suggesting that he had sent the letter to himself. The impression of a doodle that Mike Hall had found on the back of the 'You Next' note matched a doodle on a notebook found at Widden Hall Farm.

It soon emerged that Backhouse was even responsible for the car bomb that had nearly killed his wife. In early March, he had increased Margaret's life insurance from £50,000 to £100,000. The money he would have received had she died would have helped him pay off his debts.

Backhouse had launched the fake hate campaign, and a few weeks later, had

Margaret Backhouse, wife of Graham Backhouse, was badly hurt by a car bomb, planted by her husband.

planted the bomb. To escape suspicion, he decided to frame Bedale-Taylor. He persuaded him to come to his house, where he killed him, and took measures to make it look as if Bedale-Taylor had attacked him first. On the face of it, Backhouse appeared to be innocent; and it was only through patient forensic detection that the truth of his crimes emerged.

Desperate ploy

Backhouse continued to scheme even whilst in prison awaiting trial. He persuaded a fellow inmate to send an unsigned letter to a local newspaper saying that Bedale-Taylor had been responsible for the car bombing. The plot failed when the handwriting was analysed and found to be that of the prisoner. On 18 February 1985, Backhouse was convicted of murder, and sentenced to two terms of life imprisonment. This is possible because life imprisonment does not actually mean 'life' - it means that a prisoner cannot apply for parole for a minimum of 12 years.

Analysis of fibres

Every type of fibre, wool or cotton or manmade, has its own unique structure, and the type of material can be identified by examining a piece of fibre under a high-powered microscope.

For more detailed analysis — say, to match a wool fibre to a particular sweater — other methods are required, such as **infrared spectrometry**. With this technique, the degree of absorption of infrared light passing through a fibre is measured and displayed as an image. This is called a 'signature', and it can be compared to a library of other 'signatures', enabling the fibre to be identified.

Fibres can be examined under a microscope to reveal details of their shape, weave pattern and strand size.

Stolen identity

In July 1998, some Devonshire trawler men found the body of a man caught up in their fishing nets. They reported their gruesome discovery to the local police. The body was in a poor state, having been submerged for some time in 20 metres of water, and the police found nothing on the man to indicate his identity. The only clue they had was the Rolex watch on his wrist.

Rolex to the rescue

This turned out to be a lucky break, because Rolex keep records of all their customers. Inscribed inside the watch were details of when it was serviced. Through this, Rolex were able to give the police the man's name – Ronald Platt – and his address at the time the watch was serviced.

Every Rolex is traceable back to its owner.

Police made enquiries and discovered that, according to official records, Platt was still alive and well. His credit cards and bank accounts were still being used. The **forensic** team came to the conclusion that someone had killed Platt and stolen his identity. But who?

The mobile phone number

The police visited the address supplied by Rolex, and through patient detective work, eventually arrived at Platt's last known residence. The owner of the property confirmed that Platt had lodged there. He was asked for contact details of any of Platt's friends or family. He gave police the mobile phone number of a David Davies, who had provided him with a reference for Platt. When police called this number, they had no idea they were speaking to Platt's murderer.

A man of many names

David Davies was one of the names used by Albert Walker, a crooked businessman, who had swindled a lot of people out of their money, and was wanted by Interpol (an international organization of police forces). He befriended Ronald Platt, an Englishman who had spent his childhood in Canada and wished to go back there. Walker paid for Platt's return to Canada, but before he left he stole Platt's birth certificate and driving licence.

This allowed Walker to live as Platt, and he would have continued to do so if the real Platt had not decided to come back to England and live nearby. Realizing he was in danger of exposure, Walker decided to murder Platt. He persuaded him to come on board his yacht where Walker killed him. His one mistake was to leave the Rolex on Platt's wrist. Walker was convicted of murder and sentenced to life imprisonment.

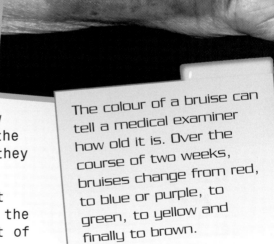

Cause of death

With the discovery of a dead body, one of the most important questions that forensic scientists must ask themselves is, 'how did he or she die?'

The Forensic Science Service, based at Chepstow in South Wales, examined the body of Ronald Platt and they found:

1 bruises on his body that covered an area exactly the same length as the shaft of the anchor

2 traces of zinc from the anchor on Platt's belt, which had been badly stretched

3 leather fibres from the belt on the anchor.

From this evidence, they deduced that the anchor had been stuffed into the belt of Platt's trousers and used to weigh him down in the water. This led them to conclude that Platt had been murdered.

The colour of a bruise can tell a medical examiner how old it is. Over the course of two weeks, bruises change from red, to blue or purple, to green, to yellow and finally to brown.

Solve it!

So, you've read the book. You've seen the professionals in action. Now solve this mystery. Imagine that you are a **forensic** scientist. You must decide which of the techniques described in the book you would use to solve the following case ...

A new drug

A dispute has arisen between two distinguished scientists. Both claim to be the inventors of a **formula** for a new drug to treat high blood pressure, which could be worth millions of pounds. In the spring of 2000, Professor Fish publishes an article describing his discovery in a scientific journal.

Shortly afterwards, Fish is sued by his former teacher, Professor Hook, who claims that *he* came up with the very same formula 15 years before, and that Professor Fish has stolen it from him. To prove it, Hook has unearthed several sheets of handwritten notes that he claims were written in 1985, describing in some detail his experiments with the drug.

The witness

To strengthen his case, Hook has also found a witness – a Ms Angler – who is willing to state in court that she assisted Hook with his experiments in 1985. Indeed, the records from the time show that a Ms Angler was a graduate student employed as a part-time laboratory assistant at the university between 1984 and 1986. The university also possesses in its **archives** a videotape of a meeting of the Chemistry Society in October 1985, at which Ms Angler delivered a paper. It includes close-ups of Ms Angler both face-on and in profile. Ms Angler left the university in 1986, and went to live abroad. All records of her cease after that point.

Is Hook a liar?

Professor Fish is outraged at Hook's assertions. He regards Hook as a jealous old rival, who is trying to steal the glory from his more talented student. He does not believe that Hook was involved in research of this nature back then, and the notes that Hook has conveniently 'rediscovered' must have been written after Fish's article was published. Even if it could be proved that the notes were written in 1985, nothing would convince him that Hook had written them himself, since – according to Fish – the man has never had an original thought in his life. As for Ms Angler, Fish has a distinct recollection of her having a longer nose, and he is certain that the person Hook is now putting forward as a witness is a different woman entirely.

What you must do

You are a private forensic investigator, hired by Professor Fish's legal team. Your job is to:

1 determine when the notes were written

2 decide whether Professor Hook wrote the notes

3 establish whether Hook's witness is indeed the same Ms Angler who assisted him in 1985.

What techniques will you use in this case?

ANSWERS

1 Identify the ink used by using a technique such as **thin-layer chromatography**. Then find out the age of the ink on the paper by measuring the quantity of **solvent** it contains using **gas chromatography**, and checking this against the evaporation curve for that particular ink.

2 Obtain a sample of Professor Hook's handwriting and compare this with the handwriting on the notes.

3 Examine stills from the videotape showing close-ups of Ms Angler in profile, and compare the shape of her ear with that of the ear of the woman claiming to be her now. Compare **spectrograms** of the two women's voices.

Glossary

archives   catalogues and items in a collection

authentication   establishing that something is genuine or true

authenticity   genuineness or truth of something

beta radiography   use of beta rays to test the density of materials, like paper. Beta rays are electrons given off during the decay of certain radioactive isotopes. They are less penetrating than X-rays, and are easily turned aside by paper fibres.

cartilage   tough, elastic tissue found in the nose, ear, throat and other parts of the body

cell   smallest independent unit in an organism

counterfeit   copy of something, especially money, made to deceive people

digital imaging technology   use of devices to convert images into digital form

digital scanner   device used to convert an image into a digital form (i.e. represented in numerical digits) in order to store, retrieve or transmit it

DNA   molecule in the form of a twisted double strand (a double helix) found in every cell of every living thing. It is a major component of chromosomes (rod-shaped structures in a cell nucleus) and carries genetic information (this determines an organism's characteristics).

DNA typing   forensic method of identifying a person by analysing their DNA

electromagnetic   created by electromagnetism, which is magnetism produced by an electric current

electrostatic   produced by static electricity, which is a stationary electric charge that builds up on an insulated object

forensic   relating to the application of science in the course of a criminal investigation

forensic analysis   detailed scientific examination for the purpose of providing evidence for use in a court of law

formula   group of chemical symbols that show what a substance consists of

fraud   crime of obtaining money or some other benefit by deliberate deception

gas chromatography   analysing the components of a gas by injecting it into the stream of another inert (non-reactive) gas and into a long, thin tube that slows down each component. As the components emerge one by one at the end of the tube, they pass through a detector that analyses them.

hoax   attempt to make people believe something is real that is not

hologram   three-dimensional image of an object

infrared part of the electromagnetic spectrum (the complete range of radiation), invisible to the human eye, consisting of radiation with wavelengths between those of light and radio waves

infrared luminescence infrared light can be used to view inks that have been erased or written over. For example, some inks that appear brightly coloured in normal light might be transparent in infrared light. In contrast, some inks, invisible in ordinary light, appear luminescent, or shiny, under infrared light. This effect, known as infrared luminescence, may be observed through a device that converts the luminescence into a visible image.

infrared spectrometry method used to measure how much infrared light is absorbed when passing through a transparent substance. This measurement, called a 'signature', can be compared to the 'signatures' of other known substances as a way of identifying the unknown substance.

investigation formal inquiry to find out as much information as possible about something

laser device that uses the ability of certain substances to absorb electromagnetic energy, which it then re-radiates as a highly focused beam of single-wavelength radiation

microprinting technique of printing text so small that it has to be magnified to be viewed

mitochondrial DNA form of DNA found in the mitochondria – the structures that produce a cell's energy. Mitochondrial DNA is harder to test than ordinary DNA and can only indicate relationships through the maternal line. However, because it is tougher than DNA from a cell nucleus, it can be found in very old remains and provides important information about archaeological finds.

Nazi Reich Marshal leading figure in the Nazi (National Socialist) regime that ruled Germany from 1933 to 1945

nucleus spherical body at the centre of a cell that contains the genetic information necessary to control cell growth and reproduction

offset printing method of printing in which inked impressions are transferred onto paper from another surface

optically variable ink ink that appears to change colour, depending on the angle from which it is viewed

pigment substance that is added to give something, such as paint or ink, its colour

questioned document any handwritten, typed or printed item that a forensic document examiner studies to assess its authenticity

scoop important piece of news that usually only one newspaper publishes

solvent substance – usually a liquid – in which other substances can be dissolved

spectrogram graphical representation of a spectrum or range, such as the range of a voice

stereoradiography process in which two X-ray photographs are taken of the same area at the same time but from different angles in order to reconstruct the shape of something such as a bone

thin-layer chromatography form of chromatography in which the components of a liquid are separated from each other. A sample of the liquid is extracted in a solvent, which is placed on a glass plate coated with a thin layer of a substance called alumina (colourless aluminium oxide). The components travel at different speeds along the glass plate because of differences in their chemical composition.

ultraviolet part of the electromagnetic spectrum (the complete range of radiation), consisting of radiation with wavelengths beyond the violet end of the visible light spectrum

voiceprint graph that shows in picture form the patterns of a voice

watermark design or mark incorporated within paper during its manufacture that can be seen when it is held up to the light

wavelength distance between two points on waves (such as radio waves or light waves) that are next to each other

wood pulp wood that has been mechanically and chemically broken down for use in making paper and paper products

X-ray high-energy electromagnetic radiation with a wavelength that is capable of penetrating solid objects

Get into forensics

Forensics is a complex and fascinating business. Investigators may be called upon to make identifications from **DNA** fragments, take fingerprints from a scene of a crime, check photographs for fakes, examine paper fibres under an electron microscope, find the age of ancient bones using radiocarbon dating, match tyre tracks left by a getaway car or compare known dental records to the corpse of an unknown person.

One person alone cannot master such a wide range of skills, and those involved in forensic investigations often perform highly specialized tasks. Ballistics experts, for example, will match projectiles with weapons and detect traces of explosives on fabric or skin. Toxicologists may be called on by a pathologist carrying out an autopsy to examine a particular organ for indications of a hard-to-detect poison.

In their way of working, all forensic investigators are scientific or medical professionals. In fact, the range of skills required is so broad it covers almost every aspect of science and medicine: physics, chemistry and biology, medicine and dentistry, anthropology, archaeology and psychology. So any reader wanting to pursue a career in this area will need to begin with some scientific qualifications.

Useful websites

Crimes and Clues: contains information about many different kinds of forensic science:
http://www.crimeandclues.com/

Questioned Documents in the Spotlight: some famous questioned document cases:
http://www.qdewill.com/cases.htm

A great site, containing case studies of different kinds of scams, frauds, hoaxes and forgeries:
http://www.sniggle.net/index.php

Further reading

True Crime Scene Investigation, Zakaria Erzinclioglu
(Andrews McMeel, 2003)

The Forensic Casebook: The Science of Crime Scene Investigation,
N. E. Genge (Ballantine, 2002)

The Forensic Science of C.S.I., Katherine Ramsland (Berkley Publishing
Group, 2001)

Index

Titles in the *Forensic Files* series include:

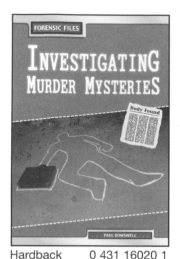

Hardback   0 431 16020 1

Hardback   0 431 16021 X

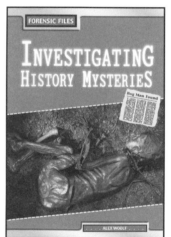

Hardback   0 431 16022 8

Hardback   0 431 16023 6

Hardback   0 431 16024 4

Hardback   0 431 16025 2

Find out about the other titles in this series on our website www.heinemann.co.uk/library